GUIDE TO FINANCIAL RESPONSIBILITY

How Does Investing Work?

Tom Streissguth

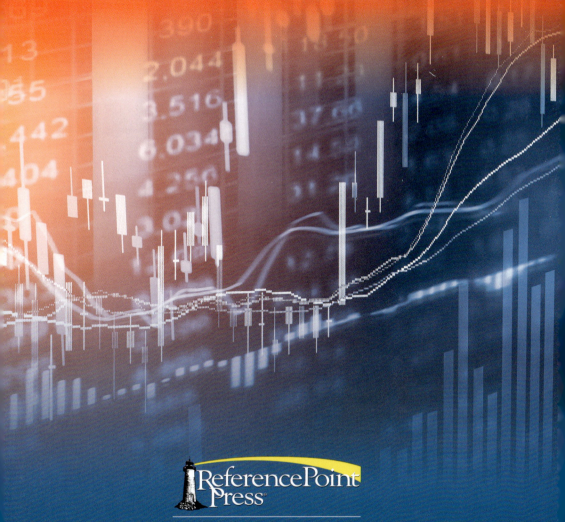

ReferencePoint Press®

San Diego, CA

© 2024 ReferencePoint Press, Inc.
Printed in the United States

For more information, contact:
ReferencePoint Press, Inc.
PO Box 27779
San Diego, CA 92198
www.ReferencePointPress.com

ALL RIGHTS RESERVED.
No part of this work covered by the copyright hereon may be reproduced or used in any form or by any means—graphic, electronic, or mechanical, including photocopying, recording, taping, web distribution, or information storage retrieval systems—without the written permission of the publisher.

LIBRARY OF CONGRESS CATALOGING-IN-PUBLICATION DATA

Names: Streissguth, Thomas, 1958- author.
Title: How does investing work? / by Tom Streissguth.
Description: San Diego, CA : ReferencePoint Press, 2024. | Series: Guide to financial responsibility | Includes bibliographical references and index.
Identifiers: LCCN 2023003899 (print) | LCCN 2023003900 (ebook) | ISBN 9781678205584 (library binding) | ISBN 9781678205591 (ebook)
Subjects: LCSH: Investments--Juvenile literature. | Saving and investment--Juvenile literature. | Stocks--Juvenile literature. | Children--Finance, Personal--Juvenile literature.
Classification: LCC HG4521 .S87 2024 (print) | LCC HG4521 (ebook) | DDC 332.6--dc23/eng/20230130
LC record available at https://lccn.loc.gov/2023003899
LC ebook record available at https://lccn.loc.gov/2023003900

CONTENTS

Introduction — 4
Knowledge Is Money

Chapter One — 7
Investing: Risks and Rewards

Chapter Two — 16
The Stock Market

Chapter Three — 25
Bonds: A Promise to Pay

Chapter Four — 34
Mutual Funds

Chapter Five — 43
Cryptocurrencies and NFTs

Source Notes — 53
Glossary — 55
For More Information — 57
Index — 59
Picture Credits — 63
About the Author — 64

INTRODUCTION

Knowledge Is Money

GameStop was once a successful and profitable video game retail business. But in the early 2000s, the company went into a slow decline. More gamers were buying their games online and not in physical stores. Malls where the stores were open were dead or dying. Instead of its regular annual profits, GameStop began losing money.

GameStop is a public company, meaning anybody can buy shares of the business. But the price of the stock was in a slow crash. Hedge funds—companies that help wealthy people invest—were betting against GameStop. They were shorting the stock by first selling shares, then waiting for the price to drop. When buying the shares back, they profited if the stock went down, not if it went up.

GameStop also attracted the attention of the WallStreet-Bets community. This was an investment group on Reddit, a news and social discussion website. In early 2021 the discussion among many WallStreetBets members turned to GameStop. A craze for the stock had begun with YouTube videos posted by a young market analyst named Keith Gill (known as Roaring Kitty on YouTube and Reddit).

Following the Crowd

Gill's YouTube channel was a popular stop for people interested in the stock market. Speaking rapidly, with price charts to back up his ideas, his GameStop video explained that "based on prevailing sentiment, the market and popular culture, many think it's a foolish investment. But everyone's wrong!"[1]

Gill urged his followers to buy GameStop shares. He talked about big hedge funds and how they were trying to drive down the stock just to make money. Their success, in Gill's opinion, would damage the company, which had long been a favorite hangout for young people. But if enough ordinary people bought GameStop stock, then the price would go up. So this wasn't just an investment idea. It was portrayed as a crusade against the wealthy and powerful people who manipulated the stock market for their own greedy ends.

Thousands of people took Gill's advice. Many young and novice investors plowed a good chunk of their savings into GameStop. They used online brokers such as Robinhood, which charges no trading fees. Short sellers had to buy back shares to avoid steep losses as the stock rose. The heavy buying took place over just a few days in January 2021, when the price of a GameStop share went from $5 to $350. Gill himself made millions as the stock rocketed into the stratosphere.

GameStop's stock price soared in early 2021 as individual traders from a Reddit group teamed up against big financial institutions.

Taking Losses

But many individual investors didn't understand the risk involved. They didn't bother to look at GameStop's financial statements, which would have told them that the company was losing revenue and closing stores. With a little research into investing history, they would also have come across an age-old scam, once known as an investment pool. In an investment pool, a group of people work together to drive the price of an asset higher. Then they agree on a date to sell, taking a profit while those outside the group watch their investments crash.

> "If you have no experience dealing with [pump-and-dumps], you will lose your money very, very quickly."[2]
>
> —James Royal, stock market expert

Those who deal in stocks have seen many such "pump-and-dumps," when stock prices climb upward on rumors and promotion by manipulators and then fall almost as quickly. One market expert, James Royal, wrote on the website Bankrate that such market manias are "tremendously dangerous for retail traders who haven't traded before. The stock can drop precipitously in a matter of seconds or minutes. If you have no experience dealing with that kind of thing, you will lose your money very, very quickly."[2]

As fast as the price of a stock can rise, it can also fall. This happened to GameStop shares, which dropped because Gill and others sold theirs in order to take a profit. The heavy selling drove the price of GameStop shares down, fast. Those who didn't sell believed they could hold on and make an even bigger profit when the stock eventually turned around. Many of them lost almost everything they had invested.

For an investor, whether such a story ends in success or failure often comes down to knowledge. As the saying goes, knowledge is power; it can also be wealth. A knowledgeable investor still takes risks but is better prepared to avoid a big loss. So investing is about knowing the markets and understanding the risks.

CHAPTER ONE

Investing: Risks and Rewards

When nobody was going out, Sophia Coffey decided to take a chance on the movies. It was early 2021, a very bad time for the cinema business. But Coffey, a student at Arizona State University, believed the movies were coming back. So she bought 185 shares of AMC, a company that operates a big nationwide chain of theaters. At the time, the stock market priced the shares at less than ten dollars each.

When the COVID-19 pandemic hit the United States in 2020, cinemas, bars, restaurants, and many other public places shut down. People stayed home for days at a time, only going out to buy necessities. If they wanted to watch a movie, they used video streaming services like Netflix. Theaters belonging to AMC closed their doors and lost money. A lot of financial experts believed the company would fail. They warned investors that buying AMC shares might well result in a total loss.

It was a risk Coffey opted to take. Still, she was a little surprised when it paid off. On one day in January 2021, AMC climbed by 300 percent to twenty dollars a share. As rumors and social media posts continued pumping the stock, it passed seventy dollars a share in May. AMC became a topic of conversation on cable TV and in investing chat rooms. AMC joined GameStop as a meme stock, one that small investors learn about through social media platforms and buy

The Saving Option

Not everybody can or wants to take risks with their money. For these individuals, a savings account or certificate of deposit (CD) offered by a bank might be the simplest option. If the bank fails, the account is insured by the Federal Deposit Insurance Corporation (FDIC). FDIC insurance means the government will return any money lost by the bank, up to $250,000 per account.

Savings accounts and CDs are good ways to keep cash safe because they are risk-free. However, the cash will lose its value over time due to inflation. The return on these savings vehicles runs 1 or 2 percent a year. If a saver puts in $1,000, the money will earn $10 or $20 every year. But in most years prices rise by a much greater amount. In 2022, for example, inflation ran as high as 9 percent. So money earning 2 percent when inflation is high is actually losing its purchasing power. At the end of the year, it buys less than it could at the beginning of the year, even if it was kept safe.

in the hopes of making a big profit. When Coffey finally sold part of her investment, it had climbed by 400 percent. Later, AMC shares dropped back down to four dollars a share. Coffey realized that buying a piece of AMC was not really investing—it was gambling. "I know some kids who are making poor investment decisions thinking they can quickly gain money," she told an interviewer for Vox. "I'm definitely not that way."[3]

Investing means doing research, forming a plan, and taking a risk. Investors have to look carefully at the financial condition of companies that interest them. They need to understand the business and think about the future. They also have to think about risk and decide how much risk they are willing to take.

In the case of AMC, the risk was very high. Instead of selling, many hopeful meme stock investors held on to their shares. They watched their investment drop from an all-time high of almost seventy-three dollars in June 2022 to four dollars by the end of the year. At that time the meme stock craze was fading, and the stock market had been dropping for a year. AMC was still a struggling movie theater company that was losing money and had a lot of debt. The difference between success or failure for AMC investors came down to research, risk management, and timing.

Investing: The Game Plan

Investors buy shares of stock or mutual funds (managed investment portfolios) for the chance of a good return on their money. They can also buy bonds, gold, real estate, cryptocurrencies, art, and many other things. All of these investments can rise or fall in value. Some investments are safe, while others are risky. Before they choose where to put their money, investors must decide how much risk they are willing to accept. In general, risky investments bring a chance at a better return—or a bigger loss.

Young people have a big advantage over adults in this game. "Age is arguably a younger investor's most valuable asset," explains Taylor Jessee, director of financial planning for Taylor Hoffman, a financial consulting firm. "This is because of compound interest, or the ability of your money to start earning its own money. . . . The earlier you start investing, the longer you'll have your money being put to work for you."[4]

Movie theaters, including this AMC branch on New York City's Upper West side, were forced to close during the COVID-19 pandemic. Some investors took the opportunity to buy the company's stock at a low price.

Young or old, everyone who takes part in the investment markets should make a plan. The first step in planning is to consider your personal money situation. If you have a job or allowance, you have income. The money can be spent on necessities, like food or clothing. It can also be spent on wants: a game, concert tickets, or a car. The money you do not spend can be saved or invested. This is discretionary money, meaning it is not needed right away. You might call it leftover money that can be put to work earning and growing on its own.

How much can your leftover money grow? It depends. Answering a question on how to make $30 billion, the most successful investor in history offered this simple advice: "Start early." It was 1999, and Warren Buffett, whose net worth at the time was about $30 billion, was speaking to the shareholders of his company, Berkshire Hathaway. "I started building this little snowball at the top of a very long hill. The trick to have a very long hill is either starting very young or living to be very old."[5]

Buffet has done both. He made his first stock investment when he was 11, buying shares of Cities Service, an oil company. When he was a teenager growing up in Omaha, Nebraska, he sold magazines door-to-door and started other small businesses. In 2022, at age ninety-two, he was still running Berkshire Hathaway, a once-struggling textile company that he bought for $14.86 a share in 1965. He turned the company into an investment firm and bought shares of other companies he thought were undervalued by the market. One of these was the insurance company Geico. Another was Coca-Cola.

At the start of 2023, Berkshire Hathaway shares were trading for $469,000 apiece. Buffet turned out to be very good at evaluating companies, figuring out which ones were cheap and taking smart risks. Over eighty years of investing, he built a personal net worth of more than $100 billion.

> "I started building this little snowball at the top of a very long hill. The trick to have a very long hill is either starting very young or living to be very old."[5]
>
> —Warren Buffet, renowned business magnate and investor

Practice Accounts

Before investing, a good idea is to practice. In a practice or "paper trading" account, brokerage customers get a credit for $10,000 or some other amount of play money. They can buy and sell anything they want. They can log in to their account to check the price of their investments and follow the news on the company.

A practice account can teach one a lot about investment and market risk. Watching prices move up and down, sometimes for no obvious reason, teaches the lesson that markets are unpredictable. Sometimes the market will go up, and the practice investments follow right along. On other days, the investments will not follow the trend. The market may go up, but the price of a single stock can still go down.

Practice accounts show how closely the price of a stock or mutual fund matches the moves in a market. A stock that seems to beat the market consistently might be a good investment in a real-money account. An investor who finds a stock behaving that way can research that company for possible investment.

Setting Goals

Before funding an investment account, an investor needs to save. This means setting up a financial safety net that will break a fall in case a job is lost or an emergency comes up. An emergency could be a serious illness, an injury, or a major car breakdown that will be expensive to repair. By definition, emergencies are unexpected. They can happen at a bad time or come in twos or threes. Smart investors set aside two or three months' income in a savings account. This gives them confidence that unexpected emergencies will not destroy their finances.

Investment accounts, on the other hand, can be used to work toward personal goals. You can use investments to save for expensive things that you need or want, such as a car or a house. Another investment goal is to create a fund for future expenses, such as a college education.

For others, the goal might be to save for retirement, or any long period when you stop working. Retirement means no money coming in from a job—and possibly no income at all. Although Social Security is available to seniors age sixty-two or older, these

Berkshire Hathaway chairman Warren Buffet speaks to reporters at an annual shareholders meeting in Omaha, Nebraska, on May 4, 2019.

payments average about $1,600 a month. In many parts of the country, this is not enough to live on. So retirees need a good amount of savings as well to afford the things they want or need.

Many jobs offer 401(k) retirement accounts. In a 401(k), some money is taken out of your paycheck and invested. Some employers also contribute to the employee's 401(k) account. Employers who do contribute typically offer to match up to a certain percentage of the paycheck. If an employee is making $1,000 a week and decides to save 5 percent, then $50 is taken out of the weekly check and put in the 401(k). A 100 percent employer match would mean another $50 is added. In all, the worker saves $100, with half of it an employer contribution.

Custodial Accounts

Starting early means starting young. But by law, young people under age eighteen cannot own property, including investment accounts. They need a parent or guardian to open the account for them. These are known as custodial or UTMA accounts, for the Uniform Transfers to Minors Act. If there is a custodial account open in your name, you are the minor beneficiary of the account, meaning the money legally belongs to you. The custodian only manages the money. When the minor reaches the age of majority, the custodial account turns into his or her personal investment account. The age of majority for UTMA accounts is twenty-one in most states and eighteen in others. In some states the custodian decides what the age of majority will be. It is important to know that the UTMA age of majority is not always the same as the legal age of majority, which applies to voting and other rights. No matter what the age of majority is, reaching it means that the custodian no longer has the right to handle the money or make new investments. The beneficiary can keep the account or close it and do whatever he or she wants with the money.

Investment Risk and Market Risk

A good way to learn about the stock market and investing is to study it for an hour a day. Good information can be found in books, magazines, and newspapers. Consumers can also find useful information on internet financial sites such as Bloomberg, CNBC, CNNMoney, *Forbes*, Kiplinger, Reuters, and the *Wall Street Journal*. There are also news aggregators, including Google Finance, MoneyCentral, and Yahoo! Finance, that link to useful and informative articles.

The key choices for an investment account come down to stocks (company shares), bonds, and mutual funds. All of these investments can lose value. The price of company shares may drop if the company has disappointing results. This is known as company risk. Also, there's sector risk. The business that the company operates in may go out of favor. Energy companies, for example, don't do well when oil prices fall. If this happens, even successful companies in the energy sector may suffer falling share prices.

Also, investors have to deal with market risk. The entire stock market can stumble if the economic news isn't good. When that happens, the shares of good companies and bad will lose their

> "My entire $5,000 in savings that took me many years to save was gone, and it was never coming back."[7]
>
> —Steve Burkholder, personal finance book author

value. The news and the stock market are hard to predict, and there is not much that individual investors can do about market risk.

Steve Burkholder grew up in an ordinary family. His parents didn't have enough money to buy him all of the sports equipment or clothes he wanted. But once he got his first job, they made him save half of everything he earned. By the time he got to college, he had $5,000 available to do with as he pleased. "One day in my junior year in college, I heard about the stock market. It sure seemed easy enough. . . . I just invest my money in a company and, I figured, after a little while it gives me back more money than I had when I started."[6]

At the time, Burkholder didn't really understand the stock market. He invested in some risky companies—and then he lost everything. "My entire $5,000 in savings that took me many years to save was gone," he writes, "and it was never coming back."[7]

Professional stockbrokers constantly study the stock market in order to make good investing choices. There are many resources that help non-professionals gain the same type of knowledge.

In time, Burkholder got his revenge. He learned about the stock market, and he put what he learned into a best-selling book for young people called *I Want More Pizza*.

In his book, Burkholder emphasizes the importance of learning to save. He suggests putting some money away with every paycheck or gift of money a young person receives. This money is kept in a bank account, safe from the ups and downs and risks of the stock market.

Time and Patience

A good way to deal with any kind of risk is to give your money plenty of time. Over years and decades, the market rises. Good companies grow, and their shares rise in price. But this process takes time, so patience is required.

Frequent trading works against patience. Jumping in and out of the market to catch short-term price movement is difficult and usually not very productive. Experts typically suggest buying and holding shares for a long time. This ensures that market drops won't destroy your savings.

Time and patience are the investor's best friends. In 2014 Charlie Munger, Warren Buffet's business partner, told a *Wall Street Journal* writer that "waiting helps you as an investor and a lot of people just can't stand to wait. If you didn't get the deferred-gratification gene, you've got to work very hard to overcome that."[8]

> "Waiting helps you as an investor and a lot of people just can't stand to wait."[8]
>
> —Charlie Munger, investor and Warren Buffet's business partner

Good investors have a lot of patience. They know they need to wait years or decades to draw out money from an investment account. That money is hard at work, so it needs to be left alone. In the meantime, the investor can always take some time to read up on the stock market, study the companies held in the account, review the plan, and set new goals.

CHAPTER TWO

The Stock Market

A market is a place to buy and sell. A stock market is a place to buy and sell stocks, which are shares in a business. If you own shares, then you own a piece of the company.

You have the right to buy more shares and keep them as long as you like. You can also sell them. When the company elects new executives, you can vote for or against them. A common experience of shareholders is to receive paper ballots in the mail or e-ballots over the internet. Shareholders use these ballots to vote for or against important decisions, such as whether the company will let another company take it over.

Big companies issue a lot of shares, so your piece of a company may be pretty small. Starbucks, for example, issued its first shares to the public in 1992. On the first day of trading, the shares cost seventeen dollars each. Over the years, the stock was split six times. A stock split means the company issues new shares, usually at a ratio of two new ones for one old one. Companies do this so that a single share is more affordable for investors who may not have a lot of money to invest.

By 2022 there were 1.2 billion shares of Starbucks available to the public. One share represented 1/1,200,000,000 of the entire company. The stock price was about $98. With the stock splits, $10,000 invested in Starbucks in 1992 would, after thirty years, be worth $4.29 million. Taken together, the company's shares were worth $113.4 billion. This is known as market capitalization—the total value of all the company's public stock.

Accounts and Trading

The first step to owning a piece of a company like Starbucks, Apple, Nike, or any publicly held company is to open a trading account. This allows the account holder to deposit money and buy shares. Investors can also keep cash in the account for future trades or just to keep in reserve.

Some stock investment accounts will offer advisors to help you select investments. Some advisors are human and others are robo-advisors. These are online bots that give advice on the right investments to buy for your age, goals, and risk tolerance. Some investment accounts are totally do-it-yourself.

There are many investing platforms on the internet, and most also have mobile platforms. Your account page will list your investments, with their current price and the value of your holdings. Every day, the page will also show whether your account is up or down for that day, and by how much.

After opening the account, investors have to start picking investments. But before putting any money at risk, get someone else's opinion on your decisions. Jim Cramer, a well-known stock picker and commentator on the financial network CNBC, claims that stock traders should "be able to explain your stock picks to someone else. That way, there's a second set of eyes on your trading decisions and you may find something you initially missed."[9]

While growing up in Toronto, Brandon Fleisher followed this advice, both at home and in school. He started investing when he was in the eighth grade, when his parents lent him some money to start trading stocks. Fleisher's math teacher had students in his class pick one stock to follow and explain their choices. Fleisher settled on a small Canadian mining company, Avalon Rare Metals. After he picked this stock, it hit an all-time high price.

His success convinced Fleisher to keep studying the stock market. He traded on paper for a few years, using practice money. Then his parents opened a real-money account for him. They funded the account with $48,000, and Fleisher turned that into

The value of Starbucks' stock has skyrocketed over the company's thirty-plus years in business. An early investment of $10,000 would be worth over $4 million today.

$147,000. He did it by choosing very small companies. A bit of good news on such companies can move their share price by a big percentage.

Fleisher also did his research. He studied the companies and dug into their financial reports. He called the companies directly and asked the executives a lot of questions. "If you didn't research a stock and its shares go down, it's your fault," he says. "A lot of people get scared out of stocks. A lot of [stocks] jump [down in value] a bit and then go back up. My advice is to do your homework and trust the numbers."[10]

Research Before Investing

No matter how careful an investor is, buying shares will always be riskier than putting money into a savings account. If a company doesn't do well, the stock will lose value. The price may never recover. In a worst-case scenario, the company might go out of business or declare bankruptcy. The stock would go to zero as investors try to sell their shares and nobody steps up to buy them. Anyone holding on, hoping the stock might recover, would then lose everything he or she invested in it.

The key to avoiding big losses when investing in a company is to do research. The first step in research is to learn what the ticker symbol for the company is. Ticker symbols represent the company name, such as SBUX for Starbucks, AAPL for Apple, or NKE for Nike. The ticker symbol is used to find data and information for the company on financial websites and to enter buy or sell orders for the shares in an investment account.

Fortunately for researchers, there's plenty of information available. Smart investors read the *Wall Street Journal*, *Forbes*, and other business publications for the latest news on the markets. Search engines on the internet can lead you to a lot of information on specific companies. By law, these companies have to publish quarterly and annual reports. They also have to update the public on important events, such as a possible sale of the company, a stock split, or the hiring of a new chief executive officer.

By clicking through a company website, you can find out how well a company did in the previous year. This information usually

> "A lot of people get scared out of stocks. A lot of [stocks] jump [down in value] a bit and then go back up. My advice is to do your homework and trust the numbers."[10]
>
> —Brandon Fleischer, young investor

Financial Reports

When studying a business's financial reports, keep in mind the three key charts that will reveal the company's financial health—or sickness. The first is the income statement. This shows how much money the company earned from the sale of its products or services. Here's what to look for: Is that number rising or falling over the previous quarter and previous year? What's the five-year trend? This statement also shows net income, meaning profit after expenses, debt payments, and taxes. The second important chart is the balance sheet. This shows the company's assets and liabilities. Here you can find how much debt the company has. Finally, there's a cash flow statement. This shows how much cash is coming in and where it's going. If cash flow is positive, then the company can invest in product research, new markets, upgraded tech systems, and more advertising. If it's negative, the company might be in financial trouble.

> "The person that turns over the most rocks wins the game. And that's always been my philosophy."[11]
>
> —Peter Lynch, manager of the Fidelity Magellan Fund

appears under an "Investor Relations" tab. You can study its financial reports and learn how much debt it has, how much it is earning in sales, and what its net profit was in the previous quarter and over the previous year. You can find out how many employees the company has and read about planned expansion into foreign markets. You can also see how well its stock shares performed in the stock market. The stock might have done better than the market average, or it might have done worse.

The effort will pay off with smarter investments. Peter Lynch, one of the best professional investment managers of all time, told an interviewer, "The person that turns over the most rocks wins the game. And that's always been my philosophy. . . . Never invest in any company before you've done the homework on the company's earnings prospects, financial condition, competitive position, plans for expansion, and so forth."[11]

How Companies Go Public

Companies that issue shares that trade on a stock market are known as public companies. That means a member of the general public can buy and sell the shares. Companies sell shares to raise the money they need to operate. They start the process by arranging an initial public offering (IPO). With an IPO, the company announces that it will be going public and listing shares on a stock market. The company sets a date the shares will begin trading. It also sets an initial target price for the shares.

IPOs get a lot of attention in the financial media, especially when an important company goes public. Investors like the idea of being one of the early shareholders in a successful company. But companies going public have to time their IPOs right. If there is a lot of public interest, many people will want to invest, and the shares will do well. If interest fades or the market is weak, the shares will drop in value. Stock prices go down when people are selling more shares than they're buying and rise when buy orders outnumber sell orders. After an IPO, the company's share prices may rise or fall. Investors who try to time these swings to make fast money can lose quite a bit.

One of the biggest IPOs in history was Facebook's, which went public in 2012. At that time, the company was doing very well. Other companies had made offers to buy Facebook. But Mark Zuckerberg, the president, didn't want to sell. In 2006 he turned down a $1 billion offer from Yahoo! He also rejected offers from Verizon and Microsoft.

A lot of pressure and attention comes with going public, so Zuckerberg kept Facebook private. But by 2012 there were already five hundred private investors who held shares in the company. In that year Zuckerberg finally decided it was time to do an IPO. On May 18 a total of 421 million shares were offered at $38 each. The IPO raised $16 billion, making it the third-largest IPO in history, after General Motors and Visa.

Before buying any stock, potential investors should carefully research a company. Earnings prospects, financial condition, competitive position, and plans for expansion may all affect a stock's future value.

On the first day of trading, the price of Facebook shares rose, then fell. The stock was volatile, meaning there were big swings in its price. By September 2012 the share price dropped by half, to below $18. Facebook shares didn't get back to the initial IPO price of $38 for sixteen months. Nine years later, in September 2021, Facebook shares were trading for ten times that amount, or $382.18. By the end of 2022 the shares were back down to $119. Investors who bought at the IPO and rode out the swings tripled their money. Investors who jumped on the stock at its peak in 2021 and then sold in 2022 lost money.

The lesson is that even big and successful companies like Facebook can be bad investments. Volatility makes it easy to lose money when trading for a short term, because the stock market is hard to predict. If you jump in and out of a stock in a short span of time, such as days or weeks, you are taking an unnecessary risk.

Trying to get in and out of the stock market—to buy when it's low and wait to sell when it's high—is a common mistake.

Day Trading Dangers

Investing can feel a bit like gambling. Investors put money at risk in order to win a good return. But some investors don't have the patience needed to succeed. Instead, they make multiple trades every day. They move quickly into and out of stocks, hoping to make a large number of small profits.

This "day trading" is stressful and difficult. Day traders follow price charts, trying to catch a small move in a stock's price as it happens. They have to watch their computers constantly when the market is open. "I like risk," says Matthew Jay, who made YouTube videos about his life as a day trader. "I'd try to jump into another stock and make some money there."

Day trading happens fast. Stocks are bought and then sold again in a few hours or minutes. But when Jay strung a few losses in a row, he found it impossible to stop. "When it's trade after trade after trade, it's that same hypnotic effect that people report when they sit in front of a slot machine." Although he had slowly built a few thousand dollars into $150,000 with patience and careful research, he lost most of that savings by day trading.

Quoted in Jim Zarroli, "Former Day Trader Warns Others of the Risk of Addiction," NPR, December 7, 2020. www.npr.org.

A big screen outside the NASDAQ stock exchange building announces Facebook's IPO at the opening bell on May 18, 2012, in New York City.

In his *Forbes* article "6 Reasons Why Market Timing Is for Suckers," contributor Jim Wang explains, "We always think we can do this successfully. The reality is most of us can't. We have no edge or advantage. It's no different than seeing a string of red numbers on a roulette wheel's history and thinking it's time to bet black."[12]

> "We always think we can [time the market] successfully. The reality is most of us can't. We have no edge or advantage."[12]
>
> —Jim Wang, personal finance writer

Stocks and Hype

When a company goes public, it has to make its financial information available. It has to give reports every quarter and every year. The reports state the amount of revenues (sales) and net income (profit). Company executives hold meetings and conference calls, during which investors can ask questions. Investors use the reports and the meetings to better understand the company's financial condition.

There can be a lot of information to take in. Public companies issue annual reports in print and digital form. Some of these run on for hundreds of pages, with charts and graphs giving all the details. Somewhere in the report may be the company's own prediction of how it will do over the next year.

On top of it all, the business media is also reporting information. Some of it is positive, some negative. A rumor reported on CNBC or in the *Wall Street Journal* can move the price of a stock fast. Small investors find it difficult to make a profit by relying on this public information. By the time they hear about it, the professional traders at banks, insurance companies, and mutual funds have already placed their orders. The higher price already reflects this activity, and then many of the pros will sell to make a profit.

This can quickly drive the share price down, and ordinary investors will probably lose money. A stock market loss like this teaches a valuable lesson: Buy stocks of strong companies for the long term, as you would a house, and don't worry about short-term swings in the price of a company's shares.

CHAPTER THREE

Bonds: A Promise to Pay

For many people, investing means buying and selling company shares in the stock market. But there are other ways to invest, and company stock is just one of many different types of investments. While a share is a small piece of a company, a bond represents debt. Bonds are used by companies and governments to borrow the money they need to operate or expand.

Companies issue bonds much like individuals take out loans, except this is usually done for different reasons. Individuals might borrow money to buy a house or a car or to pay for college. A company that borrows money might use it to build a new factory or headquarters, pay operating expenses, or buy another company.

Whether a person or a company is borrowing money, the borrower has to pay interest. The interest rate is a percentage of the loan amount. With car loans, the interest payments go to a bank or auto finance company. With bonds, the interest payments go to the bondholders. These are the people who bought the bonds, with the aim of earning income from their investment. Big, stable corporations pay low rates of interest on their bonds. They might pay 5 percent for a $10 million bond, for example. At 5 percent interest, the company pays $500,000 a year to bondholders. At the end of the bond's term, the bond matures. That means the company has to

Bonds from the Past

In the past, bonds came in the form of paper certificates. These paper bonds had the name of the company, a face amount, and the interest rate they paid. Owners had to clip small coupons from the bonds to get their interest payments.

Bearer bonds were simply bonds that could be cashed in by whoever held the bond. They weren't registered to their owners. Bearer bonds were favored by safecrackers and bank robbers, who didn't need to carry around a lot of stolen cash if they had bearer bonds.

Because they were so risky to own, bearer bonds went out of style. Now bonds are held as electronic records in a secure online database, where they are supposed to be safe from theft. Many people still collect old bond and stock certificates, however, and those issued by companies that have survived can still be cashed in.

repay the entire debt. If it's a $10 million bond that matures in ten years, then at the end of ten years the company returns $10 million (the principal amount) to the bondholders. Each bondholder receives the face amount of the bonds he or she held. At that point, the debt is paid in full. If you were holding the bond in your investment account, the account will add the bond proceeds in cash, while the bond disappears and the interest payments stop.

A company's long-term health is the most important risk involved in owning bonds. But bonds are not as risky as owning shares. On its website, the US Securities and Exchange Commission explains, "If the company runs into financial difficulties, it still has a legal obligation to make timely payments of interest and principal. The company has no similar obligation to pay dividends to shareholders. In a bankruptcy, bond investors have priority over shareholders in claims on the company's assets."[13] This means that even if the company goes bankrupt, bondholders may have some of their investment returned. Shareholders, in most cases, lose everything.

How the Bond Market Works

Most bonds come in denominations of $1,000. When a new bond hits the market, all buyers pay this price. This is known as the primary market.

Like movies and students, all bonds are graded. Rating agencies measure them for safety. The grades run from AAA (the highest rating) to D (the lowest rating). Bond investors pay close attention to ratings, because they want to know how much risk they're taking by buying a bond. Nobody wants to lose money on an investment that is supposed to be safe. Some investors buy only A-rated bonds or stick to bonds with a rating of B or better. Everybody has an investing style and has to decide how much risk is acceptable.

> "If the company runs into financial difficulties, it still has a legal obligation to make timely [bond] payments."[13]
>
> —US Securities and Exchange Commission

After the bond comes out, it trades on a secondary market. That means the price is affected by the demand for the bond. The higher the demand, the higher the price will go. The price is quoted as a percentage, not a dollar amount. That means a bond selling for 98 will cost an investor 98 percent of the original issue price. If that bond's face amount is $1,000, then buying one bond will cost $980.

If you buy a bond, you can hold it until it matures. A bond that matures is like a loan that gets paid off. The company that borrowed the money now has to pay it back, in full.

When individuals take out loans, for instance to buy a new car, they agree to pay interest—an additional percentage—on the original amount in order to repay the loan.

You can also sell the bond at any time. But most investors who buy bonds aren't interested in selling them. Instead, they keep the bonds in their accounts. They use the bonds for a stream of income. They know that every six months the bond will pay interest, in cash. They can reinvest the money or simply put it in the bank and use it for expenses.

The Risk of Bonds

The good news on bonds is they're not supposed to lose value over time. When they mature, they'll be worth the same as when they were issued. The holder of the bond will receive the face value of the bond, guaranteed. This makes bonds less risky than stocks. Bonds are for conservative investors who don't want to take chances on losing money in the stock market.

Of course, bonds still carry some risk. If a company runs into financial trouble, the value of the bonds may drop. Worse, the company might stop paying interest on its bonds. If the company goes bankrupt, the bonds might get canceled altogether. Bondholders in that case might get some of their money back, or they might not. The company might also offer them a deal for their bonds.

In early 2023 the retailer Bed Bath & Beyond ran into financial trouble. Sales were falling, and the company was losing money.

Grading Your Bonds

There are several companies that rate bonds, including the "big three" — Moody's, Standard & Poor's (S&P), and Fitch. Companies that issue bonds pay these agencies to rate the bonds. If the bonds don't have a rating, banks and other businesses won't buy them, and the bond issuance won't raise any money for the company.

Each of these rating agencies has a slightly different rating system, but in general, bond ratings are like traditional school grades. A is a high rating, B is next, and C is not so great. There are plus and minus marks used, and unlike teachers, ratings agencies can use double or triple letters. Ratings are important to investors as well as to companies that issue bonds. The lower the rating, the higher the interest rate the company will have to pay and the riskier the bond for the investor.

Running out of cash, the company decided to make a deal with bondholders. It would issue company stock in exchange for $155 million of bond debt.

The bondholders agreed, and the bonds were canceled. This maneuver saved the company interest payments. The new shareholders could sell their shares to get their investment back or hold on in hopes the company would survive and the stock price would rise. "The distressed debt exchange addresses some of the home goods retailer's debt load," explains analyst Richard Collings on the news website Axios, "perhaps buying it more time as it attempts to execute a turnaround and avoid bankruptcy."[14]

The risk of bankruptcy means some bonds pay more interest than others. Bondholders might receive 10 percent interest on the bonds of a small company and 5 percent from a US Treasury bond, which is about the safest bond you can buy. The low risk means these bonds pay relatively low interest.

Why Companies Use Bonds

Big companies need a lot of money to operate. Apple, for example, needs money to run offices, pay employees, and lease space for its retail stores. Although it gets revenue from selling phones and computers, sometimes it needs more to develop new products and services.

In 2017 the company issued bonds to borrow $1 billion. The bonds paid 3.2 percent interest. Apple paid this low rate to borrow money because it is a big company with a successful business and a lot of money. It will have no problem paying its debts, so the market sees Apple bonds as a low-risk investment. Anyone who buys one of the bonds for $1,000 receives $16 cash from Apple every six months. Two payments a year total $32, which is 3.2 percent of $1,000.

In December 2022 the bonds were quoted at 95. If you wanted to buy one Apple bond for your investment account, you'd have to pay $950. (You can buy more, of course, since there are $1 billion worth of these bonds on the market.) Since the interest payment of $32 was the same, the bonds costing $950 actually paid interest at a rate of 3.7 percent, because the interest payment represents a higher percentage of the price. This is known as the interest-rate yield. If the price of a bond falls, the interest-rate yield goes up. If the price rises, the yield goes down.

These bonds were good for ten years. In 2027 the bonds will mature and Apple will pay back all the money it borrowed. It will pay investors $1,000 cash for each bond they hold.

Government Debt and Series I Bonds

Like Apple, the federal government needs money, and lots of it. The US government has been issuing bonds since the Revolutionary War, when it used bonds to raise money to pay its soldiers. Investors can now open their own account with the US Treasury, which issues bonds for the government. With an account, an investor can loan money to the government and get paid interest.

US Treasury bonds are a safe investment. Millions of people, as well as companies and foreign governments, buy these bonds.

A lot of money is needed to run Apple's corporate headquarters in Cupertino, California (shown). Apple must pay utilities, the company's employees, and lease space for its retail stores.

As of the end of 2022, the United States had $31.3 trillion of debt. But the investors are feeling confident they'll get their interest payments on time, because the US government has always paid its debts.

The government also issues savings bonds, known as Series I bonds. You can buy these bonds online from a US Treasury website. The government adjusts the interest Series I bonds pay every six months. The rate depends on the rate of inflation. The higher the inflation rate, the higher the interest rate on these bonds.

An inflation-adjusted investment in Series I bonds keeps up with the rising cost of living. At the very worst, with rising prices, an investor will come out even but will usually come out ahead. When it comes to Series I bonds, financial guru Suze Orman is a true believer. "They come from $25 all the way up to $10,000," she told a CNBC interviewer. "So there's no excuse that all of you should not have one."[15]

States and cities also issue bonds to borrow money. These municipal bonds are paid for through the stream of taxes and fees the local government can raise. A city might need to build a public hospital or develop a stretch of land for new housing or factories. If it doesn't have the cash in the bank to pay for this expense, it can issue bonds.

The rate of interest on municipal bonds is higher than US Treasury bonds, because cities and states are riskier investments. Local governments sometimes stop making interest payments, a situation known as default. Municipal bond defaults are rare, but they do happen. The city of Detroit has defaulted on its bonds, and so has Puerto Rico. There can be many causes of a default, some of them out of a city's control. A city or county can also avoid default, or return money to bondholders, if it gets some outside help.

In 2018 a huge wildfire roared through the small town of Paradise, California. Most of the structures in the town were destroyed.

> "[Series I bonds] come from $25 all the way up to $10,000. So there's no excuse that all of you should not have one."[15]
>
> —Suze Orman, personal finance advisor

Residents and businesses were forced to move. With interest due on $5 million of municipal bonds, Paradise could no longer raise the taxes needed to pay its debt. The next step was default. In this case, however, insurance payments and financial assistance from the state of California enabled the town to avoid default. Some residents returned and rebuilt homes and businesses, and bondholders kept receiving interest payments.

Mixing It Up with Bonds

Bonds are one way to diversify your investments. This means using different types of investments for safety. Since bonds are safer than stocks, many people who are retired prefer to buy bonds. Investment pros advise adding corporate and government bonds to your portfolio as you get older. The steady income from these bonds helps pay the bills when you're no longer working. When the bonds mature, the cash you invested is returned, and you can then buy another bond.

A home burns as a wildfire rages through Paradise, California, on November 8, 2018. The town's losses prevented its paying its bondholders, but the state helped it avoid default.

The key concept is diversification. Bill Gross, also known as the Bond King, managed PIMCO Total Return, which held more than $500 billion in bond investments. Before he was a professional money manager, Gross was a professional blackjack player in Las Vegas. There he learned how to count the cards in a deck to get an advantage over the dealer. He also learned about money management and not putting all your money on a single bet.

> "You must not bet all your chips at the same time, because the results will be disastrous if you're wrong."[16]
>
> —Bill Gross, bond portfolio manager

In his book *I'm Still Standing*, Gross offers this advice: "You must not bet all your chips at the same time, because the results will be disastrous if you're wrong. . . .You don't want to own just one stock, one bond or even one piece of real estate (unless it's your home and that's what you can afford)."[16]

Diversification takes different forms. When investing in stocks, diversification means buying big, safe companies to balance the risk of smaller ones. In an investment account, it means buying bonds as well as stocks and keeping some of your money in cash. Mixing up different investments is a way to keep your account protected from a big drop in value of a single investment. It helps reduce the risk and worry of owning things that quickly change in price, sometimes from one minute to the next.

CHAPTER FOUR

Mutual Funds

Mutual funds are like investment collections that hold their assets in a big portfolio. Mutual fund companies hire fund managers, whose job is to decide which investments to buy and sell. A fund manager may buy stocks or bonds or both. The manager is responsible for keeping track of dozens, sometimes hundreds of different investments. The size of the fund is measured in the value of its assets. A big fund may have more than $100 billion worth of investments in its portfolio.

The fund manager has a big job, but he or she can't buy just anything. Every mutual fund has an investment theme that it follows, and the manager's job is to make the best possible returns while following that theme. One fund may hold only small company stocks, while another may hold corporate bonds. Funds can get pretty specialized. There are sector funds that concentrate on a single industry, like gold mining, biotechnology, or software. Some funds stick to US companies, while a global fund can invest anywhere in the world.

Lower Risk and Pro Management

Not all investors are interested in buying individual stocks or bonds. Some investors don't like the risks of the markets. They don't want to put their money into a company that might do well or might fail. They don't like the idea of possibly losing a lot of money by investing in a single company.

For these investors, mutual funds are a way to lower risk. Instead of buying shares of stock, investors buy shares

Peter Lynch, who managed the Fidelity Magellan Fund for thirteen years, is famous for his simple approach to investing.

of the fund. The price of the shares will not rise and fall all day long. Instead, the price of a mutual fund share is fixed once a day after the market closes. The total value of the portfolio, divided by the number of shares, equals the net asset value. The net asset value represents the price of a single fund share.

These shares are less volatile and less risky than shares of stock. The fund spreads the risk around all the investments that it holds. If one company in the fund falls in price, other companies in the fund may hold steady or go up. Gains will offset losses, although the fund may fall on days when the stock market as a whole is losing value. Diversifying a stock portfolio this way is the best way to lessen the risk of losing a lot of money in the market.

Another advantage to mutual funds is professional management. Choosing stocks carefully means a lot of work: studying financial reports, thinking about competitors, trying to guess how well the business will do over the next few years. If you hold shares in a mutual fund, you give all this work to someone else who is trained and experienced in this kind of research and analysis. All you need to do as a mutual fund investor is decide what kind of fund to invest in.

There are different ways to choose a mutual fund. Some investors seek out well-known or well-respected fund managers. These are people who have had great success in their job and have become stars in the financial world. One of these is Peter Lynch, who managed the Fidelity Magellan Fund for thirteen years.

Lynch is famous for his simple approach to investing. In meetings, when stock analysts brought their investment ideas to share, he would turn over a three-minute egg timer. The person talking had three minutes to explain his or her idea. "Later, he cut that time in half, to 90 seconds," explained a 2019 GuruFocus article about Lynch, "saying that if you are ready to invest in a company, you should be able to explain the opportunity in language a fifth grader would understand, and quickly enough that a fifth grader would not get bored."[17]

Getting Started

Investing in a mutual fund is pretty simple. The first step is to gather information from the fund's website. Most funds are part of a fund family, a group of different funds that are owned by a large financial company. Fidelity is the biggest such family, with 175 different funds. Other major fund companies include Vanguard, PIMCO, Franklin Templeton, Janus Henderson, American Funds, and BlackRock. Altogether, there are about seventy-five hundred mutual funds in the United States alone.

The fund's website will explain the different fund themes and offer information on each fund's performance. It is common for funds to give their average annual return over the past one, five, and ten years. The fund will also give short biographies on the fund managers and explain what the minimum investment is. A few funds have no minimums, but most set the minimum at $500 or $1,000. Each mutual fund also has to reveal how much it charges in management fees.

An investor can buy fund shares directly from the fund company, which will issue new shares and set up an account. It's also possible to buy fund shares through a brokerage account.

The most important thing to know about a mutual fund is its investment objective. Does it aim for fast growth in the share prices of stocks it holds? Or does it provide investors with a steady stream of interest income from corporate and US Treasury bonds? Does it seek out foreign companies that might do well when the US econo-

Mutual Fund Fees

When looking into mutual funds, always check management fees. These are the fees paid to the fund managers for their salaries, staff, and operating expenses. Mutual funds also charge fees for marketing and advertising expenses. Anyone who invests in a mutual fund should know the rate of fees the fund charges, because it means that the fund is paying itself that much directly from the investment.

A key statistic for any mutual fund is its expense ratio—the total amount of fees charged as a percentage of all the fund's assets. About 0.5 percent is an average expense ratio, but some funds charge 1 percent. If you invest $1,000 in a fund with a 1 percent expense ratio, then you're paying the fund $10 a year, no matter how well or how badly it performs.

my is weak? Or does it only buy large, safe multinational companies that pay dividends? By lining up your investment goals with a fund's objectives, you are more likely to be satisfied with the results.

Some mutual funds are specialized. Their investments fit a very specific theme. As one example, Fidelity has a Water Sustainability Fund that invests only in companies that deliver reliable, clean water to communities that need it. The Fidelity Agricultural Productivity Fund invests in companies that improve crop yields and grow global food production.

Sector funds are also available to investors interested in a certain type of business. There are electric car, tobacco, health care, software, utilities, banking, and real estate funds. If investors don't know a lot about individual companies, they can buy shares of a sector fund and let a professional manager worry about which companies to buy and sell. Many investors, for example, are excited about biotechnology or industrial robots. Instead of getting into all the companies that work in a sector and trying to figure out which ones make the best investments, a sector fund lets a professional do the hard work of analysis.

Bond Funds

Mutual funds also work well for bond investors. A bond fund is a big portfolio of bond investments. Instead of buying individual bonds, you buy a share of the whole portfolio. The mutual fund company hires a manager to handle all the buying and selling. You can buy fund shares through your investment account.

This saves investors all the trouble of researching and tracking individual company or government bonds. The price of the fund shares will rise and fall with the bond market, and the income from the bonds will be paid out to shareholders. These interest payments are made every month, every quarter, or every year, depending on how the mutual fund operates.

Bond funds spread the risk around. If a fund holds one hundred different investments and one of them defaults, the fund will suffer a small loss, while most of its investments will continue to make their interest payments. The big portfolio of holdings protects fund shareholders from a total loss, and the same is true of a stock mutual fund.

An electric car powers up at a rapid charging station outside a supermarket in Surrey, UK, in March 2022. Electric vehicle enthusiasts can invest in sector funds that focus on this industry.

Exchange-Traded Funds

When investors buy mutual funds, they usually make a purchase of shares from the mutual fund company or through a broker. The mutual fund creates new shares when this happens. When an investor redeems shares for cash, the fund takes the shares out of circulation.

Exchange-traded funds (ETFs) work a different way. They issue a limited number of shares, which then trade like stocks. ETFs represent a basket of different investments, like ordinary mutual funds, but their price depends on the demand for the shares. If more people want to buy than sell, the shares go up in price. If more people are selling, the price goes down. Ordinary mutual funds set a new price at the end of the trading day that depends on the total value of the fund divided by the number of shares.

There are some advantages to investing in ETFs. There's no minimum amount you have to invest—it's possible to buy a single ETF share. ETFs are managed by professionals but also charge lower fees. And these funds also diversify their holdings, so they're not as volatile and risky as stocks.

Index Funds

Many investors want to be in the stock market but don't want to search for the right stocks to buy. Nor do they want professional managers picking and choosing investments for them. In fact, most mutual funds don't beat the market averages. Even with professional management, they perform worse than the market as a whole.

The answer to this problem is an index fund. An index fund just buys all the stocks in a market index. An index follows a large group of stocks. The best known is the Dow Jones Industrial Average (DJIA), which follows thirty of the biggest companies in the United States. The S&P 500 index tracks five hundred different companies. Some of the market's biggest companies—including Amazon, Tesla, Visa, and Apple—are part of the S&P 500. Financial guru Suze Orman favors index mutual funds. On her website she states, "With one investment you become an owner of hundreds—and sometimes thousands of stocks or bonds. That's a smart way to invest. When you own just a few individual stocks

> "With one investment you become an owner of hundreds—and sometimes thousands of stocks or bonds."[18]
>
> —Suze Orman, personal finance advisor

you put yourself at greater risk, as any problem with one holding can send your entire portfolio down a lot."[18]

Market indices are considered the true measure of how well the stock market is performing. When the business media report that "the market was up today," what they really mean is that the DJIA or the S&P 500 closed higher than it did the day before. The index price changes as the prices of stocks rise and fall throughout the day. When the market closes, the index stops changing and remains the same until the market opens again.

Index funds track the market. This takes away the decision of choosing which stocks to buy. If you own shares of an index fund, you're invested in the stock market. But you're not worried about how individual companies are doing, and you're not trying to decide whether to sell the shares of one company and invest in another. Nor are you worried about how well a mutual fund manager is doing or whether you might be able to find a better one. There's no decision to make, other than how much to invest.

Index funds also save on management fees and operating costs. Since there's no manager making decisions on investments, an index fund costs much less to run. The average index fund management fee is about 0.2 percent. These savings significantly help the return on a long-term investment.

The return on your investment will equal that of the index. If the S&P is up 10 percent for the year, then an S&P index fund will match that return. Over the past 150 years, the S&P has averaged a gain of 9.6 percent a year, which is better than the return on savings accounts, bonds, and most mutual funds.

Dollar Cost Averaging

Deciding on a mutual fund is an important step. The next decision, of course, is how much money to invest and when exactly to invest it.

Visa, one of the biggest companies in the United States, is tracked by both the Dow Jones Industrial Average and the S&P 500.

There is an easy and practical answer known as dollar cost averaging. You do this by putting the same amount of money into the fund on the same day of the month, every month. A mutual fund can set this up by making regular withdrawals from your bank account or from the bank account of a custodian. Once the withdrawal is set up, there is nothing more to do except check the account statements from time to time to see how the fund is doing.

By dollar cost averaging, you buy more shares when the price of the fund is down, and fewer shares when the price is up. Over time, this means that you purchase the fund at a lower average cost and have a better chance of making gains.

By dollar cost averaging, investors don't make the mistake of trying to time the market. "Many people have attempted to time the market and buy assets when their prices appear to be low," reports *Forbes* Advisor, a respected financial website. "This sounds easy enough, in theory. In practice, it's almost impossible—even for professional stock pickers—to determine how the market will

41

> "It's almost impossible—even for professional stock pickers—to determine how the market will move over the short term."[19]
>
> —*Forbes* Advisor

move over the short term."[19] Dollar cost averaging also helps an investor avoid the stock market roller coaster, in which fear and greed cloud one's judgment and lead to poor decisions.

Investors who want to avoid the quick ups and downs of stocks and bonds can turn to mutual funds, leaving the risk-taking and tough decisions to a professional manager. Mutual funds are also ideal for new investors who might still be learning how the market works and how to evaluate individual companies.

The first decision to make is what investing theme to follow. For a younger investor, a well-run growth stock fund should beat the market over time, while an index fund will match the stock market's performance. The key is to find the investing style you're comfortable with, and buy shares of your chosen fund on a regular basis.

CHAPTER FIVE

Cryptocurrencies and NFTs

In 2008 somebody came up with the idea for a new form of money. This would be digital money that could be used in online transactions. There would be no paper notes or metal coins. There would be no governments printing the money and no physical banks loaning it out to their customers. And anyone who used the money could remain anonymous.

The inventor of this new "cryptocurrency" called it Bitcoin and identified himself or herself as Satoshi Nakamoto. To present the idea, the inventor authored a white paper—an essay that explains in detail a new or important business concept. But the identity of the writer remains a secret, because Satoshi Nakamoto has never appeared or spoken in public. A few years after inventing Bitcoin, he or she disappeared from view, leaving behind this advice: "It might make sense just to get some in case it catches on. If enough people think the same way, that becomes a self-fulfilling prophecy."[20]

Satoshi Nakamoto was right. Over the next few years, the idea did catch on. People all over the world invested in Bitcoin and other digital currencies. Crypto became one of the hottest topics in the investing world. It also proved to be a very risky investment. Many people who bought Bitcoin and other cryptocurrencies have lost a lot of money, and many of the businesses involved in this market have failed.

How Bitcoin Works

To use digital money, buyers and sellers rely on a blockchain. A blockchain is a record of digital transactions, like an online ledger. It records the amount of a transaction, and it tracks the movement of digital money from one account to another.

A blockchain is also distributed among many computers. It's a public record that in theory can't be changed or hacked. Everyone can see and verify any transaction on a blockchain. There are no banks involved in the transactions, and so there are no fees or commissions charged. The cost to carry out a transaction in digital money is less than it would be for traditional money.

But the first blockchains were not used in the sale of cars, homes, or other real-world assets. Instead, they were used to record investors buying and selling Bitcoin. Buyers set up digital wallets to hold their Bitcoin. The digital wallets were secured by a password only the user knew. This is supposed to keep the wallets safe from hackers and thieves. Unfortunately, if the user loses the password to a digital wallet, there's no record of the password

Bitcoin is a type of cryptocurrency, which means it is digital money for use in online transactions. Often depicted as an actual coin (as in this image), this currency is virtual and intangible.

The FTX Crash

To buy Bitcoin or other digital money, many investors join new exchanges. But there's little regulation of these exchanges and little control over what they can do with their customers' money. For this reason, in 2022 the crypto market faced a major crisis.

That was the year FTX, one of the largest crypto exchanges, went bankrupt. The exchange was lending its customers' assets to other crypto businesses. When the value of Bitcoin fell, the exchange began losing money—a lot of it. FTX went bankrupt, and many of its customers lost everything they had invested. More than $8 billion disappeared. The FTX disaster offers a good lesson in doing careful research not only into investments but also into the place where you buy and sell them.

online. That means the password can't be recovered and the wallet and its contents are locked forever.

New Bitcoin was "mined" by using linked computer servers to solve complex mathematical equations. As of January 2023, 19.39 million Bitcoin had been mined. The total number of Bitcoin is limited, however, to 21 million. Once that number is reached, no more Bitcoin will be mined. This limited supply is supposed to support the value of Bitcoin.

After it was invented, Bitcoin's value did rise steadily over the next few years. One Bitcoin was worth just a few dollars in 2009 but almost $60,000 in late 2021. That's a huge gain for any asset. The rising market for Bitcoin inspired many people to create new cryptocurrencies. By 2021 there were thousands of them in existence. Some rose in value, but some fell. People around the globe were buying and selling cryptocurrencies in a busy online market.

The Crypto Debate

Investors had a few problems, however. Cryptocurrency is difficult to value, since it is not associated with anything real. With dollars, for example, there's a definite number of dollars that will buy a certain amount of gold, silver, crude oil, or land. There's no way to know what one Bitcoin is really worth, since there's no way to fix its worth in the real world. How much land can you buy with a Bitcoin? Nobody knows, since it's still impossible to buy land with Bitcoin.

Another problem is that Bitcoin can be used to launder money and for other criminal acts. Laundering money involves converting money earned from illegal activities, such as drug dealing, into legal endeavors such as an ordinary business. This is supposed to hide and protect it from seizure by the authorities. Bitcoin can be bought, sold, and used anonymously, outside of the banking system and safe from police investigation.

For this reason, many important people in the investing world oppose digital currency. Charlie Munger, the vice chairman of Warren Buffet's Berkshire Hathaway company, calls it "evil." In an interview with CNBC, Munger said, "This is a very, very bad thing. The country did not need a currency that was good for kidnappers. There are people who think they've got to be on every deal that's hot. I think that's totally crazy."[21]

Nor is Warren Buffet buying the hype. "Whether [Bitcoin] goes up or down in the next year, or five or 10 years, I don't know. But the one thing I'm pretty sure of is that it doesn't produce anything," he once said. "It's got a magic to it and people have attached magic to lots of things."[22] Buffet, Munger, and other critics don't see Bitcoin as a useful form of money or an asset that's worth owning.

Others disagree, pointing out that the cryptocurrency story is still in its very early chapters. In the future, it may be very easy to use Bitcoin to buy things. Instead of pulling out a credit card, a buyer would simply open up his or her digital wallet on a smartphone. This is already possible with traditional money on mobile apps such as PayPal or Venmo.

In a crypto-accepting world, the buyer would transfer Bitcoin or another digital currency to the digital wallet of a seller. The transaction is recorded on the blockchain. If there's any dispute, the blockchain has a record of the sale that both sides can

"[Bitcoin] is a very, very bad thing. The country did not need a currency that was good for kidnappers."[21]

—Charlie Munger, vice chairman, Berkshire Hathaway

Protecting Investments

The troubles with cryptocurrencies raise an important question: how do investors know their money is safe and won't just disappear? Banks have FDIC insurance for deposits, and investments accounts have SIPC, or Securities Investor Protection Corporation. The SIPC insures brokerage customers against the loss of their stocks, bonds, mutual funds, and money. They'll pay up to $500,000 for each account, including $250,000 for any cash. It's important to remember that the SIPC doesn't protect against market losses. It only pays if the brokerage fails or goes out of business or if assets are lost through fraud.

Before putting money into any investment account, check to see whether the broker/dealer is a member of the SIPC. If you don't see the SIPC logo or acronym anywhere, call the company and ask about it. You won't have to worry about someone else's mistake—or crime—becoming your financial loss.

use. There are no banks or brokers involved. No credit cards are needed, nor do currencies from different nations need to be exchanged. It's a "peer-to-peer" transaction. It benefits both sides by being transparent and low-cost.

Investing in Bitcoin is also becoming quite easy. Online brokers such as Robinhood allow users to buy or sell Bitcoin with a few clicks or a swipe across a mobile phone screen. These platforms also offer many other digital currencies, such as Ethereum, Cardano, and Shiba Inu.

But if Bitcoin and these other cryptocurrencies were hard to actually use in the real world, why did the price of a Bitcoin keep going up and up? The answer is that people were betting with real money that it would keep going up in the future. They were buying Bitcoin and holding on to it, hoping to ride the cryptocurrency wave and make a big gain on their Bitcoin investment.

Investing in Cryptocurrency

It was 2011 when a twelve-year-old kid bored with his school in Post Falls, Idaho, heard about Bitcoin. Erik Finman decided to use the money he received from his grandmother to buy some. His got the idea from his brother Scott, who explained that the

> "I think Bitcoin definitely has more to go, and I think cryptocurrency as a whole has a lot more to go. It's the next big thing."[23]
>
> —Erik Finman, young Bitcoin investor

first Bitcoin was bought in 2010 for nine cents and that one Bitcoin was now worth twelve dollars. Finman bought about four hundred of them and waited to see what would happen.

Over the next few years Finman added to his Bitcoin collection and invested in some other digital coins, including Ethereum and Litecoin. By 2018 his Bitcoin was worth $4.9 million. He told an interviewer, "I think Bitcoin definitely has more to go, and I think cryptocurrency as a whole has a lot more to go. It's the next big thing."[23]

Finman wasn't the only person who believed in Bitcoin. New ways to invest in digital currencies became possible. Investors could buy shares in a fund that held Bitcoin, Ethereum, and other cryptocurrencies. Mining companies, which are rewarded crypto

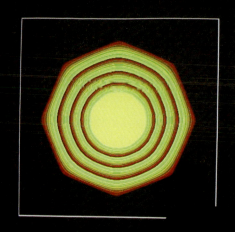

The video clip Quantum, *by Kevin McCoy, is displayed at Sotheby's auction house along with other non-fungible tokens on June 4, 2021.*

for doing complex calculations for blockchain networks, also offered shares. And then an entirely new asset was born from the crypto craze: non-fungible tokens, or NFTs.

The NFT Scene

In 2014 a digital artist named Kevin McCoy got an inspiration. He would post a short video created by his wife on the internet. He named the clip *Quantum* and offered it for sale. Since the clip was posted on a blockchain, he could track who owned it. He could also prevent any copies from being made and sold.

McCoy had just created the world's first non-fungible token. *Quantum* eventually sold for four dollars. It changed hands several times over the next few years. In 2021 an NFT collector in England named Alex Amsel, also known as Sillytuna, bought it for $1.4 million.

Something that is fungible can be replaced by a copy or another version of itself. Cash, for example, can be turned into a car, which can then be sold again for cash. Something that is non-fungible can't be replaced. It's a unique item. A digital token represents an original work of art, a design, a photograph, or a video. If it's unique and can't be replicated, it's a non-fungible token. "That day in 2014 was the culmination of a year and a half of work," McCoy later told an interviewer. "I was just thinking about how blockchains can affect and intersect with artwork . . . some people came around to the idea and built around it."[24]

Over the next few years, the market for NFTs went crazy. Many thousands were created. They represented art, music, and even tweets. Most NFTs used the Ethereum blockchain. If you wanted to buy an NFT, you used the Ethereum cryptocurrency. Many investors believed NFTs represented the future—the way that digital money would be used to buy and sell things.

Many people bought NFTs as collectors. Instead of coins or stamps or cars, they collected these digital tokens. Others bought them to speculate, meaning they were simply taking a chance that the tokens would quickly gain in value and allow them to make a profit by selling them. But since so many NFTs were being created, the value of most didn't rise. Instead of returning a profit to their owners, they did just the opposite.

Speculation Dangers

In November 2021 the price of a single Bitcoin had reached a record of $68,789. The total market value of all digital currencies was over $3 trillion. Investors carefully tracked the price of Bitcoin and other digital currencies. On the internet, they found websites dedicated to digital currencies where they could find many predictions of Bitcoin's future price. Some of these predictions seemed very confident, but they weren't backed by much research or evidence—always a danger sign. In November 2022 Srivatsa KR, an Indian contributor to *Entrepreneur*, wrote that "experts in the cryptocurrency business unanimously concur that the price of Bitcoin will most certainly reach $1 million in less than ten years."[25]

> "Experts in the cryptocurrency business unanimously concur that the price of Bitcoin will most certainly reach $1 million in less than ten years."[25]
>
> —Srivatsa KR, financial journalist

Many novice investors piled into the crypto market. Speculators bought cryptocurrencies because they believed the price of cryptocurrencies would keep going up. They didn't really have any other use for them. They still couldn't buy much with them. Just as a form of money, Bitcoin didn't work very well, because its value was so unpredictable.

Fall and Rise of the Bitcoin Market

The very first Bitcoin transaction occurred in 2010, when someone ordered a pizza for delivery in Florida and paid for it with Bitcoin. In 2021 the electric car manufacturer Tesla accepted Bitcoin as payment for a while. But the company stopped the policy when critics pointed out the harmful environmental effects of min-

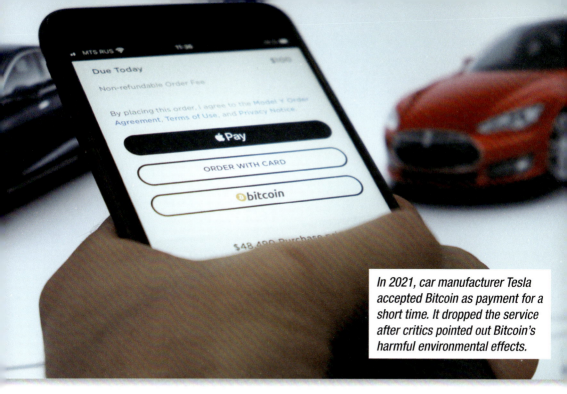

In 2021, car manufacturer Tesla accepted Bitcoin as payment for a short time. It dropped the service after critics pointed out Bitcoin's harmful environmental effects.

ing Bitcoin, which requires a lot of computing power and vast amounts of electricity.

Although speculators were still in the cryptocurrency market, many people were pointing out that Bitcoin was an unwise investment because its real-world uses were few and its value from one day to the next uncertain. Then in 2022 the market for Bitcoin crashed. The value of one Bitcoin fell to less than $20,000. The entire cryptocurrency market lost about two-thirds of its value.

But 2022 was a bad year for other kinds of investments, too. The stock market was down, and bonds also lost value. The price of gas and groceries rose, and this inflation caused rising interest rates. Higher rates are usually bad for stocks, because safer investments such as bonds will pay a better return. Many investors were selling their shares and putting the money in CDs and savings accounts. Financial experts announced the coming of a "risk-off" market, in which investors turn to safe investments, such as Treasury bonds, or simply hold cash. Taking a risk on the cryptocurrency market went out of style. Many investors sold their Bitcoin, driving the price down.

Another problem haunting the crypto market is regulation. Some governments are considering a ban on crypto ownership and trading. They also may put strict rules on crypto markets, making it harder to deal in digital currencies. Of course, governments have an interest in controlling the supply of money, and they have the power to pass laws and ban things. China banned cryptocurrencies altogether in 2013. The Chinese government also prohibited all Chinese banks from accepting Bitcoin or dealing in the Bitcoin market.

Despite the threat of regulation, by the start of 2023 the crypto market was improving. Predictions of the collapse of Bitcoin turned out to be premature. In January the price of a single Bitcoin rose from $17,000 to $23,000. The stock market was improving as well. Those who had sold their investments in the dark days of 2022 lost out. Another example was made of those who had tried to time the market. It turned out that careful research and a capacity for patience were the most valuable assets any investor could have.

SOURCE NOTES

Introduction: Knowledge Is Money

1. Roaring Kitty, *The Big Short SQUEEZE from $5 to $50? Could GameStop Stock (GME) Explode Higher?? Value Investing!*, YouTube. 2020. www.youtube.com/watch?v=alntJzg0Um4.
2. Quoted in Alicia Adamczyk, "'You Will Lose Your Money Very, Very Quickly': What Investors Need to Know About GameStop's Stock Surge," CNBC, January 27, 2021. www.cnbc.com.

Chapter One: Investing: Risks and Rewards

3. Quoted in Terry Nguyen, "What Teen Investors Learned from the GameStop Frenzy," Vox, February 10, 2021. www.vox.com.
4. Quoted in Erin Gobler, "Investing for Teens: Everything You Need to Know," The Balance, June 20, 2022. www.thebalancemoney.com.
5. Quoted in Nicolas Vega, "In 1999, Warren Buffett Was Asked What You Should Do to Get as Rich as Him—His Advice Still Applies Today," CNBC, July 23, 2021. www.cnbc.com.
6. Steve Burkholder, *I Want More Pizza*. Encinitas, CA: Overcome, 2015, p. 2
7. Burkholder, *I Want More Pizza*, p. 2.
8. Quoted in Jason Zweig, "An Interview with Charlie Munger," *Wall Street Journal*, September 12, 2014. www.wsj.com.

Chapter Two: The Stock Market

9. Quoted in Kevin Martin, "Jim Cramer Investment Advice—10 Top Recommendations," Wealth Pursuits, April 30, 2021. https://wealthpursuits.com.
10. Quoted in Karla Bowsher, "How a Teenager Tripled His Money in the Stock Market," Money Talks News, April 28, 2015. www.moneytalksnews.com.
11. Quoted in Selena Maranjian, "9 Investing Tips from Peter Lynch That You Shouldn't Ignore," Motley Fool, April 7, 2020. www.fool.com.
12. Jim Wang, "6 Reasons Why Market Timing Is for Suckers," *Forbes*, March 6, 2020. www.forbes.com.

Chapter Three: Bonds: A Promise to Pay

13. US Securities and Exchange Commission, "What Are Corporate Bonds?" www.sec.gov.
14. Richard Collings, "Bed Bath & Beyond Agrees to Debt Exchange with Bondholders," Axios, November 15, 2022. www.axios.com.

15. Quoted in Sofia Pitt, "Suze Orman: This Is the No. 1 Investment to Make Right Now, 'No Matter What,'" CNBC, June 9, 2022. www.cnbc.com.
16. Bill Gross, *I'm Still Standing: Bond King Bill Gross and the PIMCO Express*. Independently published, 2022, p. 5.

Chapter Four: Mutual Funds

17. GuruFocus, "Beating the Street: Lynch Takes Magellan to $1 Billion," Yahoo!, October 21, 2019. www.yahoo.com.
18. Suze Orman, "How to Invest for the Long Term: Keep It Simple," Suze Orman (personal website), November 21, 2018. www.suzeorman.com.
19. E. Napoletano and Benjamin Curry, "How to Invest with Dollar Cost Averaging," *Forbes* Advisor, February 10, 2022. www.forbes.com.

Chapter Five: Cryptocurrencies and NFTs

20. Quoted in Chandan Negi, "76 Interesting Satoshi Nakamoto Quotes," Internet Pillar, November 23, 2022. www.internetpillar.com.
21. Quoted in Yun Li, "Charlie Munger Says Crypto Is a Bad Combo of Fraud and Delusion—'Good for Kidnappers,'" CNBC, November 15, 2022. www.cnbc.com.
22. Quoted in Tanaya Macheel, "Warren Buffet Gives His Most Expansive Explanation for Why He Doesn't Believe in Bitcoin," CNBC, April 30, 2022. www.cnbc.com.
23. Quoted in Jeff Francis, "Meet the Teenage Dropout Who Became a Bitcoin Millionaire," Foundation for Economic Education, January 5, 2018. https://fee.org.
24. Quoted in Shante Escalante-De Mattei, "Jennifer and Kevin McCoy Bring a Cutting-Edge NFT Game to the Sundance Film Festival," ARTnews, January 25, 2022. www.artnews.com.
25. Srivatsa KR, "Can Bitcoin's Price Reach $1 Million?," *Entrepreneur*, November 10, 2022. www.cntrepreneur.com.

GLOSSARY

Bitcoin: The first digital currency, invented by a person or persons using the pseudonym Satoshi Nakamoto.

blockchain: A digital ledger that keeps track of transactions, such as the buying and selling of digital currencies and non-fungible tokens.

broker: A person or a business that buys and sells stocks, bonds, and other investments for clients.

cryptocurrency: Digital money that can be bought, sold, spent, and exchanged without the use of banks, brokers, or agents.

custodial account: An account set up for a minor, in which a parent or guardian controls the cash and investments.

dividend: A regular payment of cash by a company to its investors.

Dow Jones Industrial Average (DIJA): An index of thirty leading stocks that is used as a gauge of stock market trends.

Federal Deposit Insurance Corporation (FDIC): The federal agency that insures bank customers against loss of their accounts.

initial public offering: Also known as IPO, the first issue of shares to investors by a company that is going public.

interest: A fee charged by a lender to a borrower for a loan, measured as an annual percentage of the total amount borrowed.

market capitalization: The total value of all publicly traded shares issued by a company.

mutual fund: An investment pool that sells shares to the public and uses professional managers to buy and sell stocks and/or bonds.

non-fungible token (NFT): A unique digital representation of a creative work, such as a graphic design.

return: The increase in value of an investment, usually measured on an annual basis.

Securities Investor Protection Corporation (SIPC): The agency that insures investors against the loss of their assets through a brokerage bankruptcy or fraud.

stock split: The act of issuing multiple new shares to replace old ones, for the purpose of lowering the price of a stock and thus making it more affordable to investors.

FOR MORE INFORMATION

Books

Jasmine Brown, *The Money Club: A Teenage Guide to Financial Literacy*. Raleigh, NC: Facts for Youth, 2020.

Steve Burkholder, *I Want More Pizza*. Encinitas, CA: Overcome, 2020.

Jean Chatsky and Kathryn Tuggle, *How to Money: Your Ultimate Visual Guide to the Basics of Finance*. New York: Roaring Brook, 2022.

Bonnie J. Fernandes, *The Value of Stocks, Bonds, and Investments*. San Diego, CA: ReferencePoint, 2021.

Dylin Redling, *Investing for Kids: How to Save, Invest and Grow Money*. Emeryville, CA: Rockridge, 2020.

Internet Sources

Rob Berger, "5 Apps to Help Teens Start Investing," *Forbes*, May 8, 2022. www.forbes.com.

Matthew DiLallo, "Investment Guide for Teens and Parents of Teens," Motley Fool, January 27, 2023. www.fool.com.

Ryan Ermey, "Investing for Teens: How to Get Started," Acorns, August 25, 2022. www.acorns.com.

Erin Gobler, "Investing for Teens: Everything You Need to Know," The Balance, June 20, 2022. www.thebalancemoney.com.

Websites

Ally Invest
http://ally.com/invest
Ally is an online bank with a low-cost trading platform. Stocks, bonds, mutual funds, ETFs, and other securities can be researched and traded, and the site offers extensive investor education pages as well. Users can also research stocks with a charting tool that graphs company performance with several different parameters.

Betterment
https://betterment.com/investing

This robo-adviser site allows investing newbies to start quickly, with a custom-made ETF portfolio matched to individual resources and goals. The site charges a 0.25 percent annual fee, and when the portfolio reaches $100,000 the site allows access to certified financial advisors.

US Securities and Exchange Commission (SEC)
www.sec.gov

This government agency regulates stock markets and the securities industry. The "Education" section of the SEC site offers information on markets, investing, and the brokerage industry, as well as a section with current events and alerts of interest to the investing public. A similar SEC site for younger investors can be found at Investor.gov.

Podcasts

GenZnomics
Young Investors Society

A student-run podcast that teaches financial literacy, discusses recent market events, and offers interviews of industry leaders.

The Young Investors Podcast
Hamish Hodder, Brandon van der Kolk

Two young Australian investors discuss value investing, the idea that careful research into underpriced company shares will provide the stock market's best returns.

INDEX

Note: Boldface page numbers indicate illustrations.

age
  investment account rules about, 12–13
  investor's, and choice of mutual fund, 42
Amsel, Alex (Sillytuna), 49

bearer bonds, 26
Bitcoin
  blockchains and, 44, 46–47
  digital wallets, 44–45
  inventor of, 43
  transactions using, 50–51, **51**
blockchains, 44, 46–47
Bond King (Gross, Bill), 33
bonds
  bankruptcy of issuers and, 26, 28–29
  bearer, 26
  distressed debt exchange of, for stocks, 29
  issuance of, 29–30
  mutual funds of, 37–38
  ratings of risk, 27, 28
  stocks versus, 26, 32
  US Treasury, 29, 30–31
Burkholder, Steve, 14–15

cash flow statements of companies, 19

company risk, described, 13
company shares. *See* stocks
compound interest and age, 9
cryptocurrency
  FTX bankruptcy and, 45
  inventor of, 43
  mutual fund specializing in, 48–49
  See also Bitcoin
custodial accounts, 12–13

digital money. *See* Bitcoin; cryptocurrency
digital wallets, 44–45
diversification, 33, 35

exchange-traded funds (ETFs), 39

Facebook, 21–22, **23**
401(k) retirement accounts, 12
FTX, 45

GameStop, 4–6, **5**, 7–8
Gill, Keith (Roaring Kitty), 4–5, 6
government bonds, 29, 30–32
Gross, Bill (Bond King), 33

I'm Still Standing (Gross), 33
income statements of companies, 19
index funds, 39–40

59

inflation, savings accounts and
   CDs during, 8
information sources
   for mutual funds, 36
   for stocks, 13, 18–19, **21**
initial public offerings (IPOs)
   of Facebook, 21–22, **23**
investing
   basics of
      diversification, 33, 35
   risk and, 8, 9
investment pools, 6
I Want More Pizza (Burkholder),
   15

Lynch, Peter, 20, **35**, 35–36

market risk, described, 13–14
meme stocks, described, 7–8
mutual funds
   age of investor and fund
      choice, 42
   bond funds, 37–38
   ETFs versus, 39
   information sources for, 36
   risk of, compared to stocks, 34,
      35
   specialized
      cryptocurrency, 48–49
      index funds, 39–40
      sector funds, 34, 37, **38**

online brokers, 5, 17
Orman, Suze, 31, 39–40

"paper trading" accounts, 11
practice accounts, 11

public companies
   bankruptcy of
      bonds and, 26, 28–29
      stocks and, 18–19, 26
   financial reports of
      cash flow statements of, 19
      important sections of,
         19–20

risk
   amount willing/able to accept,
      8, 9
   company risk, 13
   market risk, 13–14
   of mutual funds compared to
      stocks, 34, 35
   ratings of bonds and, 27, 28
   sector risk, 13
"risk-off" markets, 51
Roaring Kitty (Keith Gill), 4–5, 6

savings accounts
   inflation and, 8
scams, investment pools, 6
sector funds, 34, 37, **38**
sector risk, described, 13
shares. *See* mutual funds
shorting stocks, 4, 5
Sillytuna (Alex Amsel), 49
"6 Reasons Why Market Timing Is
   for Suckers" (Wang), 23
social media platforms, 4, 7–8
stockbrokers
   online, 5, 17
   SIPC and, 47
stock market
   market risk, 13–14

"risk-off" markets, 51
ticker symbols, 19
trading accounts, 17
stocks
  bankruptcy of companies and, 18–19, 26
  bonds versus, 26, 32
  distressed debt exchange of bonds for, 29
  meme, 7–8
  researching, 13, 18–19, **21**
  risk of losing value, 13–14
  risk of mutual funds compared to, 34, 35
  shorting, 4, 5

trading
  accounts to enable, 17

Tesla, 50–51, **51**
ticker symbols, 19
trading accounts, 17

US Treasury bonds, 29, 30–31
UTMA (Uniform Transfers to Minors Act) accounts, 12–13

Wang, Jim, 23

YouTube, Gill and GameStop on, 4

PICTURE CREDITS

Cover: Dean Drobot/Shutterstock.com

5: TY Lim/Shutterstock.com
9: Rblfmr/Shutterstock.com
12: Reuters/Alamy Stock Photo
14: Standret/Shutterstock.com
18: Mats Wiklund/Shutterstock.com
21: fizkes/Shutterstock.com
23: Lev radin/Shutterstock.com
27: UfaBizPhoto/Shutterstock.com
30: Variya Zankovych/Shutterstock.com
32: Associated Press
35: Reuters/Alamy Stock Photo
38: LSP EM/Shutterstock.com
41: Kikinunchi/Shutterstock.com
44: Julia Tsokur/Shutterstock.com
48: UPI/Alamy Stock Photo
51: Justlight/Shutterstock.com

ABOUT THE AUTHOR

Tom Streissguth has been writing nonfiction books for the school and library market for three decades and has more than one hundred books in print in the areas of history, biography, geography, and current events. He has worked as a teacher, editor, and journalist and is also the founder of the Archive, a reference collection of historic journalism by leading American authors, including Ernest Hemingway, Mark Twain, H.L. Mencken, Nellie Bly, Lincoln Steffens, Damon Runyon, and Ida Tarbell. His previous titles for Reference-Point Press include *The Art of Anime and Manga* and *Biotech Careers*.